Preface

This is the first in a series of short volumes covering different aspects of the history of Ayscoughfee Hall. Future planned titles include the Household of Ayscoughfee Hall, the history of Ayscoughfee Gardens, the later history of Ayscoughfee Hall and the collection of objects owned by the Johnson family.

Introduction

Ayscoughfee Hall is one of the most important medieval town houses in Britain and has Grade I listed status[1]. And yet for all its significance, it remains little known. Whereas other important houses from the same period have had major studies published about them, Ayscoughfee has been sadly neglected[2]. This may in part be due to long standing confusion over the date when it was originally built, or the many architectural styles that can be seen in the Hall. Whatever the reason, recent reappraisals and new evidence allow us to now tell the story of this wonderful building.

For all the later additions and alterations, Ayscoughfee Hall is a profoundly medieval structure. This was a period when few could read or write, when individuals thought differently from us about the world and when religion was of central importance to people's lives. Medieval people acquired information in different ways than we do today. Signs, symbols and even buildings conveyed subtle messages about whom to respect and who was powerful. Ayscoughfee was no exception to these delicate promptings as we shall see.

Background

The 1450s was a turbulent decade in England's history. King Henry VI occupied the throne, a man who experienced periods of severe mental and physical difficulties during his life. His reign had seen the continuation of the Hundred Years War with France and the divisive and tumultuous Wars of the Roses was about to begin.

It was also during the 1450s that a group of men began to cut down the several dozen oak trees that eventually formed the roof of Ayscoughfee Hall[3].

What sights would have met the people who began to build the Hall at that time? It is likely that they would have found a well established community in the area, one that dated back to Saxon times. Pieces of pottery from the ninth century were found north of Spalding parish church in 2006, while material of a similar date was excavated from the 2008 digs in Ayscoughfee Gardens. So there is good evidence that the high ground occupied by Ayscoughfee and the church had been inhabited for many years by the 1450s. Settlements concentrated on high ground is a pattern replicated in many places across Britain; early people may have perceived these areas

as safer and more defendable than the surrounding spaces. Perhaps too, an area of high ground appealed to people living in the low lying Fens with all the attendant problems of flooding. The position next to the church would also have been considered a prestigious one.

The Domesday Book lends credence to this theory of a settlement on the Ayscoughfee site. It records that there were three manors in Spalding; one of these was owned by Crowland Abbey and another by a Norman named Ivo Taillebois. These were both on the west side of the Welland. The third, long unidentified, was owned by a man named Guy de Craon and has been tentatively identified as the Ayscoughfee site. Little is known about him, but Craon is a town in north western France and so this may indicate his family had a connection to that area.

Both Ivo and Guy are among those reputed to have travelled to England with William on his voyage of conquest in 1066. A relative of Ivo's features later in this story.

The Hall

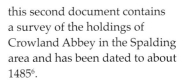

In the collection of Lincolnshire Archives, there is an account roll covering the year from September 1478 to September 1479[4]. Often kept for tax or administrative purposes, an account roll recorded revenues from or expenditure upon specific pieces of land. This particular document was compiled by a man named John Clony, a rent collector for the Abbot of Crowland. There is a complementary document in the Library of Cambridge University[5];

Below: The boundary wall from trench three (see plan on page 6), looking south.

this second document contains a survey of the holdings of Crowland Abbey in the Spalding area and has been dated to about 1485[6].

Between them, these two documents make it clear that a *berehowse* (an inn or tavern) once stood on the site of Ayscoughfee Hall. They also show that even during this early period, the Hall was known as *Aiscoughall*.

Perhaps the berehowse was part of the settlement that dated back to Saxon times, or perhaps it was more recent than this. It is also possible that the inn and maybe even some other buildings were cleared away to make room for what became Ayscoughfee Hall. During the excavations in 2008, two trenches were opened on the south lawn in Ayscoughfee Gardens. One of these revealed an enormous wall, aligned east to west, which was tentatively dated to the late medieval period, the time when the Hall was built.

The size of the wall has led to speculation that it once formed a boundary between two separate properties that were ultimately joined to form the present five acre site of the Gardens. The wall appears to be aligned with a sight deviation in the boundary wall that runs parallel to the River Welland; the deviation bows

The doorway in mid-air

This blocked doorway is to be found on the south wall of the room in the tower that has been identified as the private bedchamber of the master of the Hall. Its odd position gives further credence to the idea that another building once stood on the site now occupied by Ayscoughfee Hall. Three facts are obvious: firstly, it is a doorway as hinges are clearly visible on the right hand side and a catch of some kind can be seen on the left. Secondly, it was not used for very long, as the steps are unworn and the stonemason's chisel marks can clearly be seen. Finally, the steps are at the same level as the landing in the stair hall outside the room.

One theory to explain the doorway's presence and location is that the building that once stood on the site of the Hall was dismantled at the same time as the present Hall was being built; perhaps some of the old building materials were even reused in the new structure. If this is correct, the doorway may have been one way in which the two adjacent building sites were linked. This goes some way to explaining why the steps have so little wear: they would not have been used very often, as the period when both building sites were operating simultaneously would have been relatively short. It is also interesting to speculate why the doorway was retained in the new structure. Perhaps the method of building meant that it could not be removed or filled in, or it may even be that the Hall's new owner thought of it as an interesting feature and wanted it to be left as it was!

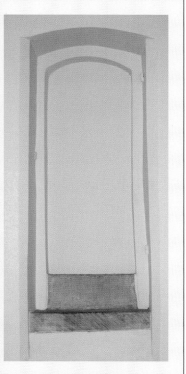

Above: *The doorway in mid-air. It is actually about a yard above the present level of the room's floor.*

out to the meet the southern end of the wall surrounding the forecourt in front of the Museum. Although the excavated boundary wall is too large to have formed part of a building, it is more evidence of substantial human activity in the Ayscoughfee area, activity which was all but erased when the present Hall was built.

Further evidence to support this idea comes in the form of the many pottery sherds discovered during the 2008 excavations in Ayscoughfee Gardens.

The earliest date from the Saxon era, but types dating from the early medieval period and made at potteries in Stamford, St. Neots in Cambridgeshire and Bourne regularly appeared, and are typical of the wares used by people in this area and during this period[7].

Evidence of occupation continues into the fifteenth century. British sherds came from East Anglia and the Midlands, while other vessels had been imported from Germany, The Netherlands and Valencia.

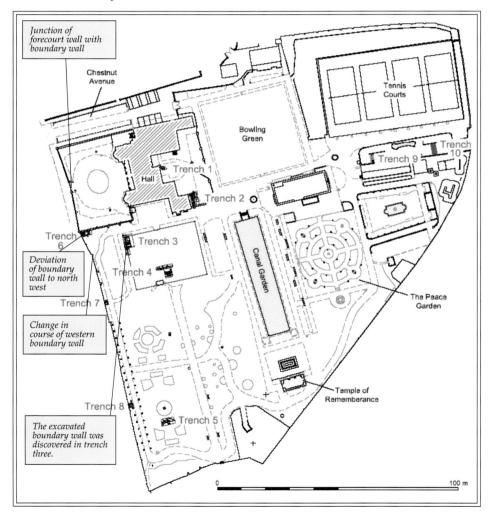

Junction of forecourt wall with boundary wall

Chestnut Avenue

Tennis Courts

Bowling Green

Trench 1

Hall

Trench 2

Trench 9

Trench 10

Trench 6

Trench 3

Deviation of boundary wall to north west

Trench 4

Canal Garden

Trench 7

The Peace Garden

Change in course of western boundary wall

Trench 8

Temple of Rememberance

Trench 5

The excavated boundary wall was discovered in trench three.

0   100 m

Building the Hall

Building a hall like Ayscoughfee, in fact building any substantial structure in the medieval period, was a huge undertaking. Nothing is known about the men who built the Hall, but from the surviving evidence of other building projects of this period, some facts are clear. The entire scheme would have been overseen by a master mason, who is best thought of as the equivalent of a modern architect. He would have marked the building's plan on the ground, and may also have produced drawings and even wooden models of the elevations or specific features for his workers to follow. Unfortunately none of these survive for Ayscoughfee, and there are actually very few for most British medieval buildings.

The building site would have had many similarities to a modern operation: wooden cranes would have been used to move timber, bricks, mortar and stone to higher levels, and the workmen would have used timber scaffolding lashed together with rope.

What made this particular project even more complex was that Ayscoughfee was to be made of brick. Although bricks were not a new technology (they were probably introduced to this country by the Romans), bricks made in Britain were an innovation, as the majority of building projects using bricks normally obtained them from the Continent. Even the word itself was new: the earliest reference to *brykes* dates to the early fifteenth century; until this point bricks are known simply as *tiles* or *waltyle*.

Not only was brick a new technology, it was also an expensive one. At the time Ayscoughfee was built, the use of brick was associated with prestigious buildings that only the very wealthy could afford. Specialists had to be employed to make the bricks and considerable amounts of raw materials were required for the process, the main one being, of course, clay. Geologically, much of eastern England is comprised of clay, and therefore it is not a coincidence that many significant fifteenth century building projects in the region, and particularly Lincolnshire, used bricks.

Ayscoughfee should not be seen in isolation from these developments in the technology and use of brick, but rather at the centre of them. We are also fortunate that although no records survive from the building of Ayscoughfee, there are documents from a

Note the use of scaffolding, hand tools and a crane in this image. The low roofed building that can be seen in the background on the left was known as the lodge. This is the area where the workmen ate and kept their tools; it was also where raw materials were prepared before being taken to the building site itself. It may even have served as a dormitory.

The illustrations on these pages also indicate something else of great importance: the influence exerted by the owner over the finished building's design and layout. It is not co-incidental that the individuals who initiated these projects are shown prominently here. The large amounts of money required for materials and wages meant that the owner would probably have had significant control over the finished building, although this input would most likely have been at a non-technical level.

These thirteenth century images of a building site again show extensive use of hand tools for shaping and finishing wood and brick, as well as a crane, wheelbarrow and brick hod. The man second from left in the top image is the master mason, in charge of the building project. Medieval master masons were traditionally represented carrying the tools of their trade, namely the set square for checking right angles and the dividers for measuring dimensions.

contemporary structure, also made predominantly of brick and also in Lincolnshire, that provide a valuable comparison. That building is Tattershall Castle[8].

Tattershall was built by Ralph, the third Lord Cromwell between 1434 and 1446. It is the only one that still remains of a large group of buildings that once formed an entire estate and was created as Cromwell's private residence. The documents show that Tattersall's master mason was

Tattershall Castle

probably a man named Bawdwin Docheman or Baldwin Dutchman; ironically Baldwin was not Dutch as Docheman in the medieval period referred to someone from Germany or northern Europe.

Baldwin was clearly a clever man, as not only did he oversee the scheme, but he also arranged to provide the bricks with which it was built. The sheer scale of the Tattershall building project can best be shown by listing the numbers of bricks that he supplied. Between 1445 and 1446, he prepared 384,000 large bricks and 84,000 smaller ones; this was in addition to 274,000 that he had made the previous year and were yet to be used.

It is clear from the surviving accounts that Baldwin's work was lucrative: even though he was dead by about 1458, his widow was paid £11 13s. 4d. for making a further 160,000 bricks. The clay used to make the bricks came from clay pits on Edlington Moor near Woodhall Spa and was fired in kilns owned by Lord Cromwell at Boston and Edlington Moor.

The arrangements for brick production at Tattershall were replicated at other building projects. There were few commercial brickyards at this time, so temporary "clamps" (as opposed to permanent kilns) were often created close to the building site. A clamp consisted of a large amount of dried, unfired bricks

Although these images of brick clamps date from the eighteenth or nineteenth century, they contain elements that would be recognisable to medieval builders. The large piles of bricks are what remains after the fuel had burnt off. Note also the use of wheelbarrows and horse-drawn carts to transport the bricks to where they are needed.

completely surrounded with fuel comprising twigs, branches, hedge cuttings and undergrowth. The whole construction was covered with clay in order to retain the heat generated by the burning fuel, as this allowed the bricks to fire. This process was difficult to control, primarily due to the inability to regulate the heat, and many bricks would have been lost or rendered unsuitable during firing.

The Tattershall documents also shed light on the amount of other material and labour required for a building of this size, the sums needed to pay for it and the areas from which it came. Iron was transported from Spain and the Baltic and was obtained through the port of Boston; wood for the kilns that fired the bricks was sourced in Stixwould, eight miles from Tattershall; the quarry at Wilsford near Sleaford supplied stone, and pre-prepared glass for the windows was bought in Boston. Money was also spent on transporting these items to where they were needed and paying workmen to use them.

It is very likely that had the accounts for Ayscoughfee survived, they would show similar expenditure on a similar range of materials. Perhaps also Ayscoughfee's master mason was Flemish or German, rather than British.

11

This fifteenth century Flemish image shows the process of brick making at a permanent kiln rather than a temporary clamp, but there are other elements which are relevant to Ayscoughfee. A man kneads the clay in the centre background before it is placed in the wooden moulds on the left to assume a rectangular shape and to dry. They are then placed in the kiln (the building in the background on the right), for firing. The bright red finished bricks can be seen on the extreme right.

Brick was not the only material used in Ayscoughfee. Stone too played a large part in the construction as, unlike brick, it does not splinter when it is shaped and dressed. The Hall's window surrounds, mullions and moulded doorways were all made of stone.

There is no indication where the stone used at Ayscoughfee came from, although it is known that stone from the Ancaster quarries near Sleaford was used at Tattershall[9]. However, the cost of transporting stone was high so the ideal situation was always to locate a quarry as close as possible to the building site. Where it was impossible to do this, quarries often supplied stone pre-prepared to the master mason's specifications on a commercial basis. This was particularly the case with ornate elements like string courses or plain ones like window and door surrounds.

One of the most impressive features of Ayscoughfee Hall is the roof. Each of the three main sections of the building (the main hall and the north and south wings), has its own style of roof construction. There was no structural or engineering need for them to be different to each other; the only reason they are is because the builder could afford to have each made differently and thereby take another opportunity to demonstrate his wealth.

Visitors to the Hall today are able to see only part of the roof above the great hall, whereas until the Georgian alterations in the 1790s nearly all of each of the three roofs would have been fully visible. The complexity and workmanship of each would have been very apparent to everyone, exactly the effect desired by the owner.

The roof space above the former great hall has many features of interest. Carpenters' marks can be seen near the apex of many of the rafters that comprise the roof's thirty arches. Carpenters often marked the timbers they were working on in order to remind them where they were to be used in the building. In Ayscoughfee's case, Roman numerals were used to indicate the sequence in which the individual rafters were to be positioned, but they are entirely random with no discernable pattern. This may indicate that a series of rafters or even entire trusses were hauled into position at the top of the building until one was found that happened to have the correct dimensions.

Near the centre of the roof is evidence of the opening that once allowed the smoke from the hearth in the great hall to escape. This was blocked with re-used timber, and it has been suggested that this may originally have been used in the louvre that once covered the opening.

The roof above the north wing is made up of forty-seven minor trusses scissor braced and collared, while that of the south wing has had a lath and plaster partition inserted about a third of the way along from the west front of the Hall. The roof structure from the front to the partition is impressive and well finished, although it underwent some repair in the early seventeenth century. Like the rest of the roofs at Ayscoughfee, it was clearly designed to be seen from below. The rest of the roof is much cruder in appearance and probably indicates that it was hidden by a suspended ceiling, never intended to be seen. This gives credence to a theory concerning the purpose of this space, an idea discussed in more detail below.

The roof is also important to the history of Ayscoughfee for another reason, as it allowed the building to be accurately dated for the first time. A total of 34 thin cylindrical samples were taken from various timbers in all three sections of the roof in 2003. These showed that the timbers from which they were taken were felled in 1451. Most importantly, the dating proved that the Hall was built in one campaign which is highly unusual for a building project of this period[10].

Although we do not know what material was used to cover

Dendrochronology, or the science of tree-ring dating

As they grow, most species of tree produce a ring of new wood around their circumference. The width of these rings usually varies from year to year, depending on the age of the tree and the climate and conditions in which it grows. It was an early twentieth century American scientist named A.E. Douglass who pioneered the technique of counting these rings in order to establish the age of a particular piece of timber.

Knowing the number of rings is clearly not enough to establish a particular age however, as this information must be compared to a sample of wood that has already been dated. These comparisons are made with timber samples known as long master sequences; the rings in the master sequences are literally lined up alongside those of the piece of wood to be dated until the width of the rings in both samples matches exactly.

The amount of work involved in dating a sample can occasionally be reduced, as specific, large-scale environmental events cause trees to add rings of an instantly recognisable width. The floods of 1947 throughout southern Britain caused abnormally wide growth rings, for example. Similarly, the amount of atmospheric ash produced by the Tunguska meteorite explosion of 1908 meant that most trees in northern Europe barely grew at all during that year, and gave rise to narrow rings.

This is a view of one of Ayscoughfee's roof spaces. That they remain substantially unchanged from the 1450s to the present day allowed for the entire building to be accurately dated for the first time in 2003.

Long master sequences exist for only a few species of tree, but one of these is the European oak. Ayscoughfee's oak roof beams were compared with samples taken from a house on Church Street in Crowland which had themselves been dated by comparison with the European oak master sequence. The dating process revealed many similarities between the samples; this, and also the cost of transporting wood in the medieval period, suggests that the oak used in both buildings was sourced locally.

Ayscoughfee's roofs, it is unlikely to have been thatch. Medieval builders had a number of roofing options available to them, and thatch was the cheapest of these. It is improbable that the original owner would have spent so much on his new home, only to have roofed it in the cheapest material available. A thatched roof was also the most vulnerable to fire and this makes it even more likely to have been rejected.

Slates from Cornwall and Devon, tiles made from fired clay or stone, and oak shingles are all possibilities, and there is evidence that these materials were in use during this period. Ceramic tiles, or *thaktyle*, seems the most likely choice, as these could probably have been obtained from the same source as the bricks. Their use would also have served to further emphasise the owner's wealth.

More evidence of the original builder's affluence was the inclusion of an undercroft. The building historian Anthony Quiney has written that "The fireproof qualities of a semi-subterranean building constructed of stone were particularly valuable, as was the more general security offered by such a strong building. Undercrofts were therefore well suited to the storage of those goods where security from fire and theft was paramount."[11] Having an undercroft also meant having high-status items to store within it, more proof of the builder's significance.

The position of the undercroft within the Hall gives further weight to its importance. The north wing of the building was where the family had its private apartments, and it is likely that only honoured guests would have been allowed into this space and therefore to see the undercroft's valuable contents. Niches are still visible in some of the arches that may have held wooden shelves which displayed these precious items.

It is not known how many men were employed to build the Hall. Surviving records from other British medieval building projects show that numbers varied considerably as the scheme progressed. It is also not known where the workers came from. Perhaps local labour was utilised or the use of brick as a specialist building material meant that men with previous experience had to be called upon. Tattershall Castle's accounts from 1434 – 1435 record that the large sum of £50 13s 10½d was paid for "Wages of masons called Brekemasons. To various masons called brekemasons and their servants engaged on different kinds of work at the same place for the period of the account."

Ayscoughfee Hall
in its architectural context

Ayscoughfee Hall is one of a number of surviving late medieval brick buildings still to be found in Lincolnshire. A substantial comparison has already been made with Tattershall Castle, but there are others that should be mentioned. Gainsborough Old Hall (Gainsborough), Hussey Tower (Boston), Rochford Tower (Fishtoft) and the Tower on the Moor (Woodhall Spa; this was also built by Ralph, Lord Cromwell of Tattershall), were all constructed at about the same time as Ayscoughfee by individuals intent on using architecture to draw attention to themselves and their influence, status and power: each building was a bold, self confident statement.

It is interesting to speculate whether the builders of these structures knew one another and

*Gainsborough
Old Hall*

influenced the respective designs in any way. Certainly Richard Benyngton, collector of taxes and Justice of the Peace for Boston and builder of Hussey Tower, knew Cromwell, and Tattershall has been described as the "immediate inspiration"[12] for both Hussey and Rochford towers. Thomas Burgh, the builder of Gainsborough Old Hall, was a member of the royal court and would have moved in Cromwell's circle; as the Sheriff of Lincolnshire in 1460, he would have known of Tattershall Castle. Indeed given that medieval Lincolnshire has been described as "one of the most isolated of English shires"[13], and rarely received royal visits, it is improbable that men of comparable rank and standing in the county did not know of each other, or at the very least of their activities.

There are further links. The loose grouping of traders known as the Hanseatic League, although based in northern Europe and the Baltic States, had extensive links with eastern England. The port of Boston saw a great deal of Hansa activity in the thirteenth century: a monument to a Hansa merchant, Wisselus de Smalenburgh, and dating from 1312, can still be seen in St. Botolph's church. They undoubtedly contributed to making the town's annual fair one of the most important in the entire country; records show that many London merchants made the long journey to Lincolnshire to attend the fair, such was its significance in the mercantile calendar. Many Hansa ports, particularly on the Continent, had warehouses, offices and weighouses, and these were often made of brick. Perhaps this European influence led the Guild of the Blessed St. Mary to build Boston's magnificent Guildhall in about 1390.

These influences also extend to domestic architecture. It is known that at least five men of high rank who fought under Henry V against the French, and who probably saw high status buildings made from brick, returned to England and built structures out of the same material. Lord Cromwell of Tattershall was one of these men, while Sir John Falstof (immortalised as Sir John Falstaff by Shakespeare), was another.

We have seen that Tattershall's master mason was probably from the Continent and had experience of making and using bricks, and contemporary records show that others with similar skills also travelled from northern Europe to satisfy the demand of those who wanted to use this new, high-status material for their building projects.

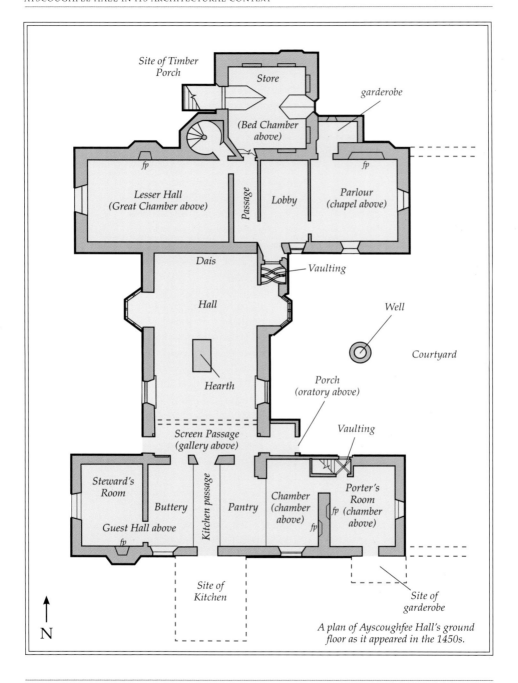

Site of Timber Porch

Store

garderobe

(Bed Chamber above)

fp

Lesser Hall
(Great Chamber above)

Passage

Lobby

Parlour
(chapel above)

fp

Dais

Vaulting

Hall

Well

Courtyard

Hearth

Porch
(oratory above)

Vaulting

Screen Passage
(gallery above)

Steward's Room

Buttery

Kitchen passage

Pantry

Chamber
(chamber above)

fp

Porter's Room
(chamber above)

Guest Hall above

fp

fp

Site of Kitchen

Site of garderobe

N

A plan of Ayscoughfee Hall's ground floor as it appeared in the 1450s.

The structure and layout of the Hall

Ayscoughfee is typical of the grand homes that were built during this period. It has a traditional H-shaped structure, with two wings flanking a central hall. The great hall is one of the oldest features in English domestic architecture: it dates back to Saxon times, and it was actually to endure until the Stuart period.

Wings began to be added to this traditional pattern in the fifteenth century (this once again emphasises how strikingly modern Ayscoughfee would have been when it was first built), one of which was used for the owner's family's private chambers, the other for services like food preparation and storage. In Ayscoughfee's case, these were the north and south wings respectively.

Ayscoughfee's great hall measures approximately 36 feet long by 24 feet wide, a ratio of 3:2. This dimensional relationship developed in the fourteenth century and lasted until the sixteenth, and shows that the Hall's master mason was aware of the period's architectural styles and trends[14].

Note that only one entrance led to the north wing from the hall and it appears on the far right of the illustration on page 20. It gave access, via a short passage with a beautiful ceiling of vaulted brick, to the spiral staircase in the tower and thus to all the rooms used by the family.

The tower contained two bedrooms, one for the master of the house and the other for his wife. It is possible that the large room at the front of the building (referred to as the Great Chamber in the line drawing on page 18), was subdivided in some way to provide private bed chambers for the owner's family.

The illustration on page 20 also reveals another of the Hall's secrets: the squint or spy hole. Situated high up on the east of the first floor, the squint gave an excellent view of the entrance below and allowed the master and family of the house to see those arriving at the Hall.

The southern end of the great hall would have been dominated by a screens passage. This was a wooden screen that spanned the entire width of the hall, and was primarily designed to obscure the activities of servants from the gaze of the people dining

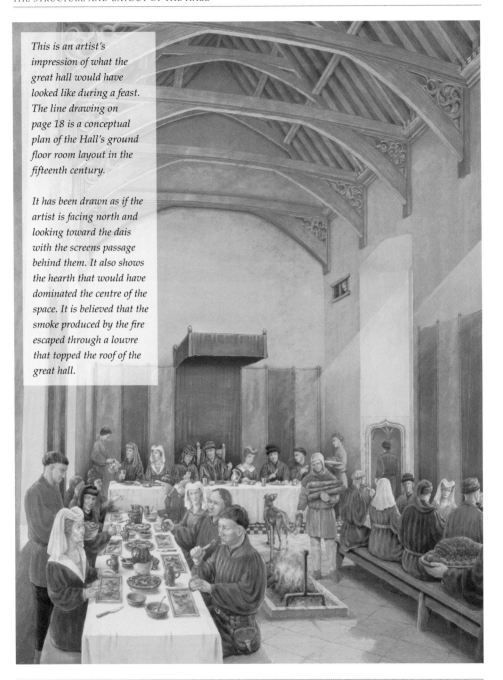

This is an artist's impression of what the great hall would have looked like during a feast. The line drawing on page 18 is a conceptual plan of the Hall's ground floor room layout in the fifteenth century.

It has been drawn as if the artist is facing north and looking toward the dais with the screens passage behind them. It also shows the hearth that would have dominated the centre of the space. It is believed that the smoke produced by the fire escaped through a louvre that topped the roof of the great hall.

in the hall. Early medieval examples of these structures were often designed to be moveable, but Ayscoughfee's was built to be permanent as it also served two other functions. Firstly, the position of the main entrance to the entire Hall behind the screen meant that only those visitors specifically sanctioned to do so were allowed into the great hall and beyond. In a feudal society dominated by status,

The roundel

The sculpted roundel is one of the Hall's most fascinating and mysterious features. It shows a group of five figures in a variety of poses. No-one today can be sure what it means, but this is not surprising as it was intended for a medieval, not modern, audience. The almost universal illiteracy of medieval people meant that information was imparted to them and assimilated by them in a very different manner than that of today. For example, no medieval person visiting Ayscoughfee would have been left in any doubt that those on the dais at the northern end of the great hall, bathed in the sunlight coming through the oriel windows, were people of importance and high status. Perhaps the best clue to the roundel's true meaning is its position. It is located near the entrance that led to rooms on the first floor that were purposely set aside as a communal dormitory. Access would have been gained via a stone staircase (now partially demolished), beneath a splendid vaulted brick ceiling, a surviving combination that is thought to be unique in the medieval architecture of the British Isles. Those gaining entrance would have probably taken advantage of a small chapel or oratory located on the right at the top of the stairs, to give thanks for a safe journey and arrival. They would have been given a plain straw bed and simple food because providing these things was seen as a worthy act of goodness on the part of the wealthy, all too concerned about the ultimate fate of their immortal souls. Perhaps some of those who took advantage of this hospitality were pilgrims. One of the individuals on the roundel, the man on the extreme left, displays the medieval iconography typically associated with such travellers: he carries a travelling bag over his shoulder and there is a space on his cap for a pilgrim badge.

it is possible to see the screen as a symbolic as well as a physical barrier.

The second function was that the screen acted as a structural support for the musicians' gallery, which was located above it on the first floor. The combination of the gallery's high position allied to the full height of the roof space would have made Ayscoughfee's acoustics very good indeed.

The original oak beam to which the screen was attached and from which it was suspended remains in its original position and can still be seen.

The screen had openings in it that led to doorways into the south wing, and the line drawing on page 18 shows how the ground floor of this space was divided.

Two of the three original stone entrances to the buttery, kitchen passage and pantry still survive at Ayscoughfee; that of the buttery is still in its original position, while the second (possibly that of the pantry), has been moved.

The kitchen may have been housed in a detached building located centrally on the south wing. Although no physical evidence remains to support this suggestion, kitchens were hazardous places given their reliance on exposed fires for cooking. Placing these dangerous facilities as far as possible from the private chambers of the owner's family probably represented the best compromise for incorporating them in the Hall.

The origins

One important question remains to be answered: who was responsible for building Ayscoughfee Hall? Tradition has long held that it was a wool merchant named Richard Aldwyn[15]. Certainly a successful wool merchant would have had access to the substantial funds necessary to build Ayscoughfee. Wool in the medieval period was an incredibly lucrative commodity. When he was imprisoned by the Duke of Austria in 1192 on his return from the third crusade, at least part of the huge ransom demanded for King Richard I's release was paid in bundles of wool. The industry's significance is also remembered in the Woolsack, the seat of the Lord Speaker in the House of Lords.

English wool merchants had the natural advantage that wool from this country was regarded as the finest in Europe, and was the most sought after by continental weavers. In 1454, a merchant would have paid about seven marks per sack for wool from South Holland; this was about half what the finest wools from Shropshire or Leominster were worth[16].

Little is known about Richard Aldwyn, although various sources describe him as a merchant of the staple[17]. The staple was a town or place, ordained by the king, in which a group of merchants were given exclusive rights to trade certain types of goods; the word also referred to the merchants themselves, as their trading rights were granted by the monarch. The staple for wool was based in Calais for much of the medieval period.

This arrangement was mutually beneficial: the merchants enjoyed the support and protection of the king, and he was able to use the Staple "as an instrument of royal finance, by which the Crown was able to obtain large sums of money on credit."[18]

The traditional link between Ayscoughfee and Richard Aldwyn appears to date back to 1846, for it was in this year that a Spalding well excavator named "Old" Robin Harmstone published "Notices of remarkable events and curious facts with various interesting scraps, connected with the history and antiquities of Spalding in the county of Lincoln, and the places adjacent." The reference in this book appears to be the first time that Aldwyn was identified as the builder of Ayscoughfee Hall, although the story itself may be much older.

The will of Richard's son,

Sir Nicholas (who certainly was a wool merchant), gives further credence to this idea[19]. The will was made in 1505 and Nicholas died in the following year[20]. It is a substantial document, befitting a man who became Lord Mayor of London in 1499. It lists many bequests to trusted friends and servants and makes suitable provision for the care of his immortal soul through the saying of masses, as would be expected for a man of Nicholas' standing. It also set aside sums to allow for the repair of some of the bridges in the South Holland district that he would have used on his journeys between Spalding and London, most of which would have been undertaken in connection with his business dealings. Travelling was difficult and arduous in the medieval period and the will's provisions for repairs serves to emphasise this.

The will makes it clear that although Nicholas never forgot his connections with Lincolnshire, he was also profoundly conscious of the significance of his life in London. Between it and the archives of the Mercers' Company,

Medieval religious guilds

Religious guilds are not to be confused with trade guilds. The purpose of the latter was to protect the work of local craftsmen by drawing up regulations covering all aspects of their trade. Religious guilds were fraternities of wealthy men and women "who came together for their mutual benefit by promoting acts of charity and welfare"[21]. This included making provision for the local poor or the saying of masses for the souls of departed guild members; anything in fact, that would reduce the time the Roman Catholic Church told them they would have to spend in Purgatory as part of the penance they would have to do for the sins they had committed in life.

Guilds were finally abolished in the 1540s when King Henry VIII created the Church of England during the English Reformation. For Catholics, the notion of Purgatory as a realm where the souls of the dead were judged and punished according to their conduct during life was actually to persist until 1999 when Pope John Paul II described it as a state of existence and not as a physical place.

Most towns had guilds. Spalding had at least three (Holyrood, St. John's and Trinity), and Cowbit one (also named Trinity); Sir Nicholas Aldwyn was a member of each except Holyrood.

Most guilds had chapels specifically for their use in the local church, but the wealthier organisations were able to pay for guildhalls to be built. The Guild of St. Mary's Guildhall in Boston is one such building. Erected in the 1390s, this guildhall employed thirteen beadsmen to say masses for deceased members, as well as providing a space for its affiliates to celebrate the many feasts held on saints days.

*The first page
of Nicholas
Aldwyn's will.*

we learn that from 1451 to 1452, he was initially apprenticed to John Broddesworth[22], a man who appears to have taken on many apprentices during his career as a merchant. Nicholas appears to have approved of such a policy as he took on a dozen of his own during his career.

What little is known about the life of an apprentice mercer can be gleaned from a close study of the few surviving documents that describe the arrangements they had with their masters[23]. An apprenticeship could begin when the apprentice was anywhere between ten and sixteen years of age, and lasted for between seven and ten years. Nicholas spent ten years as an apprentice and was admitted to the Mercers' Company in about 1463.

Most agreements between master and apprentice provided food, lodging and training in return for service. Some arrangements prohibited marriage or imposed a curfew, others included the supply of clothing. Although little is known about the true nature of an apprentice's duties, it is very likely that they all learned to deal with customers and suppliers. Any variety in their experiences must have depended on the nature of their master's work. An apprentice helping to run a stall in a London market would have lived a different life to someone apprenticed to a master who participated in European trading or dealt with the Crown.

Upon reaching adulthood and working as a mercer in his own right, much of Nicholas' activities appear to centre on the Cheapside area of London, which is just to the east of the present day St. Paul's Cathedral and north of the Thames. It was appropriate for Nicholas to find himself here as Cheapside was a place of trading dating back to at least the early medieval period. He lived on nearby Coleman Street, and had links to the churches of St. Mary Magdalene on Milk Street and St. Mary-le-Bow (which is itself on Cheapside), both of which were in easy walking distance of his home. His will makes considerable provision for the funeral service to accompany his burial at St. Mary-le-Bow.

Also in close proximity were the Guildhall (which remains the official residence of the City of London Corporation) and the Mercers' Hall where Nicholas would have spent much of his time meeting his fellow merchants and discussing the events of the day.

The Mercers' records show that Nicholas had an active career with them. In November 1479 for example, he was asked to ride to the Lords at Westminster with the Mercers' answer to a request from King Henry VI for a subsidy of £2,000. Whatever information Nicholas gave to the Lords appears to have been unacceptable, as in January 1480 the Mercers asked him to devise a means of pleasing the King about the subsidy. This instruction apparently gave Nicholas little room for manoeuvre, as February of the same year saw him appointing a solicitor to arrange for the subsidy's payment.

In retrospect, it was inevitable that Aldwyn, upon assuming a prominent position in the Mercers' Company, would move in government circles. The huge sums of money generated by trade meant that merchants, and particularly wool merchants, "could not remain aloof from the political struggles of fifteenth century England"[24], struggles that culminated in the Wars of the Roses.

Reference has already been made to the wealth of information contained in Nicholas' will, but the document is also important for another reason as in it he refers to "his grete place in Spalding". This has long been regarded as a reference to Ayscoughfee Hall, but other evidence supports a different interpretation.

The document in Cambridge University's Library referred to earlier indicates that Ayscoughfee Hall was owned successively between 1478 and 1485 by Reginald and John Gayton, presumably father and son.

Reginald was a Gentry Justice of the Peace for the Holland district of Lincolnshire in 1471, and acted in this capacity until at least 1493. He was therefore a person of some standing. John was a chaplain and a substantial land owner in the Spalding area, some of which, including the Ayscoughfee site, he inherited from Reginald.

We also know that a large home stood next door to Ayscoughfee Hall for many years and bore their family name. Gayton House[25] was demolished in 1959, but just before the end, a report was compiled about it by Mr. T.W. Townsend (a member

Taken together, these images clearly show that Gayton House was every bit as grand a building as Ayscoughfee Hall. The fine carved detailing above the doorway and the substantial roof indicate that it was meant to impress. The exterior view shows the house following its Georgian remodelling in the eighteenth century

of the Spalding Gentlemen's Society) with the aid of Mr. W.G. Prosser of the National Buildings Record (now part of the National Monuments Record, itself part of English Heritage).

Did the Bishop of Lincoln visit Ayscoughfee Hall in 1486?

In his book "A history of Spalding"[26], E.H. Gooch claims that John Russell, Bishop of Lincoln and Lord Chancellor of England (c1430 – 1494), consecrated a private chapel in the Hall on 11th May 1486. He says that this was combined with a visit to Cowbit on the same day, when the church there was reconsecrated.

No proof has been found that the visit to Ayscoughfee took place. The Lincoln Episcopal register[27] for Russell's tenure as Bishop confirms the visit to Cowbit, but there is no mention of a journey to Spalding also on the 11th. These documents were compiled by a registrar and acted in part as a diary but also as a record of decisions made by the bishop, as well as judgements relating to legal matters: anything, essentially, that the registrar considered worthy of inclusion and that he believed may be useful in the future. We can be certain not everything was recorded so it is quite possible that Bishop Russell did visit Ayscoughfee, but that it was thought to be of insufficient importance to be entered into the register.

Consequently if Gooch is correct, he obviously consulted some other primary material. However, he makes it clear in the introduction to his book that it was compiled "from many other sources which I cannot now recall"[28], so it is possible that the basis for this claim may never be found.

Like Ayscoughfee, the house was large (it had fifteen rooms) and built of brick, but only up to the level of the first floor. Above this, timber uprights with horizontal lath or wattle between them were used; these were covered in mud and plaster.

They dated the building to 1500, and their report makes clear that it was a very substantial residence and can only have been built by a wealthy family. It would certainly not have looked out of place alongside Ayscoughfee Hall.

Comparing the evidence of the Gaytons' involvement with the traditional theory produces a few difficulties, not least that the Gaytons' ownership of Ayscoughfee would have to have occurred between the time the Hall was built by Richard in the 1450s and owned by Nicholas, presumably in the very late 1400s or early 1500s. There is no evidence to support either Richard's disposal of the Hall (for whatever reason), or its reacquisition by Nicholas.

A better explanation for the origins of the Hall would appear to be that it was not built by the Aldwyns but by another family altogether, and a possible candidate does exist.

The Ayscoughs

Sir William Ayscough was one of the famous Ayscough family who hailed from Stallingborough in the north of Lincolnshire[29]. Little is known about his family's origins, but the name appears to derive from the old Norse for oak wood or oak hill.

Sir William chose the law as his profession, and spent much of his career acting as an official in the Court of the Common Pleas. It was so named as it dealt with suits that did not involve the king; its main business was the recovery of debt.

He began as a Sergeant at Law in 1438. The Sergeant's role in the Court was to plead his client's case in front of the Justices. This was a period when cases were heard in the Court without juries, so it was the Justices who decided on the matters brought before them. Sir William became a Justice himself in 1440, and remained so until 1454.

The period of training required to become a Sergeant was a long one: Sir William seems to have taken eight years to reach this position, and others took even longer. Sergeants were invited to take up the office by the king and there were severe penalties if the post was refused. The main reason for rejecting the request was one of cost. Becoming a Sergeant entailed a celebration lasting four days, which was paid for by the new office holder. Additional expenses included the provision of a feast for other court officials, the purchase of the robes he would wear as a Sergeant and the provision of gifts of gold rings for all those attending the celebrations, as well as many of the realm's nobles.

The main reason for aspiring to become a Sergeant (and possibly a Justice), and the expenditure of such large sums was that the "Law as a career offered excellent opportunities for the accumulation of landed wealth".[30] It has been pointed out that "Almost every transaction in the court or its offices involved the payment of a fee to one or more officers".[31] It was from the receipt of these fees that the members of the legal profession made their money, and although it has proved impossible from surviving records to estimate what their total annual income would have been, it is clear that considerable fortunes were made.

Only a Sergeant at Law was allowed to plead a case in the Court of the Common Pleas. This professional monopoly had in

This c1460 scene of a court in session in Westminster Great Hall would have been very familiar to Sir William Ayscough. The seven men at the back, dressed in red, are the Justices. In front of them is a large table with nine men seated around it. These are the clerks of the Court, three of them Chief Clerks each with two assistants. They make a record of the Court's activities on the rolls of parchment that can be seen in front of them. Two men appear to stand at either end of the table; they both carry a staff in their right hand. These are the Court's criers and they call the proceedings to order. All the men standing in the foreground wearing blue and green robes are Sergeants at Law. Note how they, like the Justices, are wearing white coifs (a close fitting skull-cap of cloth), as a mark of their office. An echo of this garment can be found in the wigs that barristers and judges still wear. The bare legged, long haired individual with his back to us has been identified as a debtor brought from Fleet Prison to answer charges at the Court.

part been created through the use of a language called law French. When beginning to present his case in front of the Justices, the Sergeant would read his opening statement in a rapid, law French monotone, and the Sergeant for the other party would have to follow this speech to ensure that all the details were correct. Other documents used by the Court were in Latin, still others in English. Such arrangements were maintained in order to preserve the practice of law for the few.

Despite the opportunities open to him, Sir William was dissatisfied with his situation. In June 1441, he wrote to Henry VI pointing out that as he had been a Sergeant for only two years before becoming a Justice, "all his Wynnings that he sholde have hade in the said office of Sergeant and alle the fees that he had in England weere and be cessed and expired fro hym to his grete empovysshyng for they weere the grete substance of his lyvelode"[32].

However, given that Sir William remained a Justice for fourteen years and that he received an annual salary of 150 marks[32], as well as an income from fees, it is clear that he was a wealthy man.

Sir William had a connection with Lincolnshire, because by 1446, he had become Commissioner of the Peace for the county[34]. However the last reference to him holding this office is in 1452 and his final year as a Justice was 1454, so it is possible that he would have had the time needed to oversee the immensely complicated building project the result of which was Ayscoughfee Hall.

Sir William's death in 1456[35] means that he may not have lived to see the completion of the Hall, but the activities of his son John give further support to the Ayscough family's influence in this area at the time Ayscoughfee was built. Sometime during the 1460s John married a woman named Margaret Tallbois. Margaret was a member of the family descended from Ivo Taillebois, the man who was granted lands in this part of Lincolnshire by William the Conqueror. Perhaps the Ayscoughs saw a marriage with a member of the ancient Taillebois family as a dynastic and symbolic one, cementing ties with land owners of long-standing, while simultaneously emphasising their links to this area.

There is certainly an indication that Margaret was a landowner in her own right, as a document in the National Archives shows that she held land in Spalding, Pinchbeck and Gosberkirk[36].

It is important to speculate why Ayscough, a man with no known connection to

Spalding, would decide to build Ayscoughfee Hall in the town. It is possible that his decision sheds light on a very important element of the building's history: the name. The word Ayscoughfee was occasionally written as "Ayscough fee"; it is referred to as such on John Grundy's 1732 map of Spalding and Richard Everard's watercolour of the Hall from about 1790, thus emphasising both the name of the possible builders and the word fee.

The role of a fee was well established in the early medieval period. It was an estate in land, known as a manor, held on condition of homage and service (usually military in nature), to a superior lord by whom the manor was granted and in whom the ownership remained. The most basic and common form of military service was to provide a fighting man when required by the superior lord. These men were knights, and this is why fees are sometimes known as knights' fees.

By the 1450s when Ayscoughfee Hall was built however, the concepts underpinning the fees of the early medieval period were archaic. No longer were those holding manors expected to provide fighting men for their superior lords, but this did not prevent the manors themselves still being

occasionally known as fees. This echo of an earlier age may have been exactly what attracted Sir William to the Ayscoughfee site, as he would have known the status of a piece of land associated with an early medieval fee. Its acquisition would have had the dual benefit of implying antiquity and gravitas, but also had little practical contemporary significance or associated responsibilities. Alternatively, and with the same benefits and for the same reasons, he could have created the title himself by combining his surname with the ancient legal device of a fee.

Either of these methods amounts to a splendid piece of self-promotion, and linking this with Ayscough's personal connections and Ayscoughfee Hall itself, shows that Sir William was determined to improve his status in society. Valid links can easily be made between his aspirations and those of Sir Thomas Burgh, the builder of Gainsborough Old Hall, who as we have seen, was a member of the royal court.

It is not known who owned the Ayscoughfee site just before the Hall was built; perhaps it was in the possession of a member of the gentry, an absentee landlord or even the Church. Spalding Priory and Crowland Abbey both owned land in the town, and the proximity of the Parish Church may even have meant that it had acquired the land sometime between the eleventh and fifteenth centuries.

There is no direct evidence that the Ayscoughs were responsible for building Ayscoughfee Hall, just as there is no evidence that the Aldwyns were responsible either. Also, assuming that the Ayscoughs did build the Hall, it is not known how or even if the ownership passed directly to the Gaytons, or whether other owners intervened.

What is certain is that the Aldwyns did own a grand home in Spalding; Sir Nicholas refers directly to it in his will. But what if this was not Ayscoughfee as has been supposed, but somewhere else entirely?

Could it instead have been Gayton House?

We now know that the Gaytons owned Ayscoughfee from about 1478 to 1485. It is possible that when they vacated Gayton House to move into Ayscoughfee, the Aldwyns moved into Gayton House. We have seen that Gayton House was a grand residence, certainly on a par with Ayscoughfee, so it would definitely have merited the description "grete place". Moreover, there is evidence that there were other links between the Gaytons and the Aldwyns. Nicholas' will makes provision

for a religious service to be given in the names of his mother and father, and also a man named Robert Gayton. Although it is not known if Robert was related to either Reginald or John Gayton (or even if he was still alive at the time the will was written), the common surname suggests that he was linked in some way. This evidence of good relations between the two families might have extended to what amounted to a reorganisation of their domestic arrangements.

The Gayton's ownership of Ayscoughfee during the late 1470s to about 1485 also makes it easier to understand and explain what happened afterward, as the Hall stayed in the family's hands until 1602[37].

A man named William Hall, a member of a Nottinghamshire family, married one of Reginald Gayton's descendants. They had a son named Simon, and he married a woman named Julian (sic) Roberts of Donington. Their only child was named Reginald, and he inherited Ayscoughfee Hall when his father Simon died in either 1565 or 1566[38]. Reginald's first son, Robert, sold the Hall to Thomas Wimberley in 1602.

Conclusion

The great gulf of time between the modern world and the mid fifteenth century camouflages the four hundred years between what is thought to be the first recorded mention of the Ayscoughfee site in the Domesday Book of the 1080s, and the 1450s when the Hall was built. The lack of documentary evidence from this long period means that some of our questions will probably always remained unanswered. What is clear however is that when it was finished, Ayscoughfee Hall would have been an astonishing building and very few people would have seen anything like it. It still has that same power to astonish today.

Bibliography

Many primary source materials, published works and individuals have been consulted in the process of writing this book, but apart from those referenced in the footnotes, restrictions of space prevent them from all being listed here. The publishers will be happy to supply a complete bibliography upon request; please contact the Museum directly to obtain a copy.

Acknowledgments

My thanks are due to all those individuals with whom I discussed specific sections of the guide book's text, and particularly to those at South Holland District Council and Classic Printers, Crowland (especially Philip Green and Simon Emery), who were involved in its production. Additionally, I am grateful to those institutions and individuals who allowed me to reproduce their work or items from their collections in the publication, or those who rendered their assistance generally. These are the British Library; the Board of Trinity College, Dublin; The National Trust; Michael Elsden of Spalding; the Spalding Gentlemen's Society; Andrew Watts of Stoke-On-Trent; English Heritage; all of the helpful and assiduous staff at Spalding Library; FAS Heritage; NAU Archaeology; Inner Temple Library, London and Querceus Ltd. I would also like to record my particular gratitude to Julia Knight, Ayscoughfee Hall Museum's Museum Officer, for her ideas, encouragement, support and refreshments.

Author: Richard Davies
former Manager of Ayscoughfee Hall Museum

Printed and Designed by Classic Printers Ltd., Crowland.

1   The importance of Ayscoughfee Hall was recognised by English Heritage in 2012, when its listed status was raised from Grade II to Grade I. This rightly places the Hall in the top 25% of the country's most important historic structures.

2   The Marquis Curzon and H. Avray Tipping's study of Tattershall Castle was published by Jonathan Cape of London and appeared in 1929, while the investigation of Gainsborough Old Hall edited by Philip Lindley was published by The Society of Lincolnshire History and Archaeology in 1991.

3   Personal communication with Robert Howard of the Nottingham Tree-ring Dating Laboratory, 2009.

4   Lincolnshire Archives 6 Anc. 5/1.

5   Cambridge University Library Additional MS. 4400, ff 54 – 60.

6   Information on both these documents has been obtained from H.E. Hallam's article "The agrarian economy of south Lincolnshire in the mid-fifteenth century" (Nottingham Medieval Studies, volume 2, 1967, pages 86 – 95), and via communication with the relevant repositories.

7   J.G Hurst's article "Medieval and post-medieval pottery imported into Lincolnshire" in the book *Land, people and landscapes*, (Lincoln 1991), ed. Dinah Tyszka et al., shows that the pottery found at Ayscoughfee was unexceptional and exactly the type of material that a site with this history of occupation would have been expected to produce.

8   Information for this section of the guide book is taken from W. Douglas Simpson's book *The building accounts of Tattershall Castle*, Lincoln Record Society 55 (Hereford, 1960).

9   The other great local quarry dating from the medieval period was at Barnack near Stamford. Barnack stone was used to build the cathedrals at Peterborough and Ely. It is thought that supplies were exhausted by about 1460, so it is possible that the stone used to build Ayscoughfee was sourced there.

10 Pers. comm., Robert Howard.

11 Anthony Quiney *Town houses of medieval Britain*, (New Haven and London, 2003).

12 Anthony Emery *Greater medieval houses of England and Wales 1300 – 1500*, Volume II, (Cambridge, 1996), "Rochford Tower".

13 Gerald Hodgett *Tudor Lincolnshire*, History of Lincolnshire volume VI, (Lincoln, 1975).

14 The information on ratios of great halls is taken from Margaret Wood *The English mediaeval house*, (London, reissued edition, 1994).

15 A number of different spellings of this surname have been recorded, including Alwyn, Ailwyn, Alwyne, Allewyn and Oldwyn. The single variant Aldwyn has been chosen for convenience.

16 One mark was the equivalent of two-thirds of a pound sterling.

17 Very little original information still exists about medieval merchants, many documents having been lost in the Great Fire of London in 1666. It is known that Richard Aldwyn was not a member of the Drapers' or the Mercers' Company, and probably not a member of the Worshipful Company of Woolmen or the Haberdashers Livery Company either. Merchant companies (organisations that protected the rights and interests of those trading in particular goods), were all based in England's capital. Most of the companies still exist and are now charitable organisations.

18 W. I. Haward "The relations between the Lancastrian government and the merchants of the staple from 1449 to 1461", in *Studies in English trade in the fifteenth century*, ed. Eileen Power and M.M. Postan (London, reissued edition, 1966).

19 Sir Nicholas was definitely a member of the Mercers' Company.

20 The will is part of the collection of the National Archives and has been catalogued as PRO prob/11/15.

21 Quiney, ibid.

22 There are also many spellings of this name. Broddesworth was arrested in about 1450, and Nicholas' apprenticeship was transferred to another mercer named Richard Rich.

23 I am greatly indebted to Donna Marshall, Assistant Archivist of the Mercers' Company, for the information upon which this section is based. Any errors in interpretation are my own.

24 E.E. Rich *The Ordinance Book of the Merchants of the Staple*, (Cambridge, 1937).

25 Gayton House later became known as Holyrood House (possibly because the remains of the hall of the mediaeval Holy Rood Guild stood behind it until at least 1888), and then Fairfax House.

26 E.H. Gooch *A history of Spalding*, (Spalding, 1940).

27 Lincolnshire Archives, Lincoln Episcopal registers, register 22 (Russell's register).

28 Gooch, ibid.

29 This William Ayscough should not be confused with the William Ayscough, Bishop of Salisbury, who was murdered by a mob in Wiltshire in 1450. Bishop William was probably Sir William's great uncle.

30 Margaret Hastings *The court of common pleas in fifteenth century England*, (New York, 1947).

31 Hastings, ibid.

32 *Archæologia*, xvi. 2 (1812, pages 3 – 4). This letter was written from the home of John Stafford, who became Chancellor of England in 1432 and Archbishop of Canterbury in 1443. The acquaintance of such an important man only serves to emphasise Ayscough's connections. Stafford had also trained as a lawyer and this is perhaps how the two men met.

33 All Justices also received an allowance for their robes three times a year.

34 The purpose of this office was to oversee the provision of the king's justice in a given county.

35 He was buried in Bedale Church, Yorkshire; interestingly, there is a hamlet nearby named Aiskew. As with the Aldwyns, the family's surname was spelt in many different ways over the years.

36 Document reference number SC 8/85/4219; Margaret's surname is spelt as Askew.

37 Information for this section of the guide book is taken from A.R. Maddison's book *Lincolnshire Pedigrees*, Volume II, (London, 1903).

38 Maddison (ibid) states that Reginald Hall (the son of Julian and Simon), inherited Ayscoughfee Hall from his mother. It is believed that this is incorrect, as there is no evidence to suggest that Julian's family, the Roberts, had any connection with Ayscoughfee prior to her marriage to Simon. There is considerable evidence however to suggest a link by descent and marriage between the Gaytons and the Hall family.